SPARK:
THE COLORING BOOK
For the Radically Authentic Life

MICHELLE A. VANDEPAS

SPARK: The Coloring Book

Copyright © 2017 by Michelle Vandepas

All Rights Reserved

Published in the United States of America
by GracePoint Matrix, LLC Publishing Division

theSpark.love

For further information, contact support@gracepointmatrix.com

All images are either unique or used under license from providers such as shutterstock.com.

ISBN: 978-0-9724686-7-1

The images in this book have been printed on one side of the page to minimize bleed-through. For some types of media, you may want to insert a blank piece of paper between pages. This allows you to use the art materials of your choice. We suggest colored pencils and gel pens. Other choices are markers, crayons, pastels or pens. Experiment with tools and techniques to achieve the look you want. Enjoy the Journey!

Sign up here for bonus material, discounts, tips, and see sample pages from other people:

theSpark.love

Join the Facebook group here: https://www.facebook.com/groups/thespark.love/

As you spend your time in creative contemplation with this book I encourage you to allow the images to speak to your Soul and connect you with the energy of your Inner Spark. My book designer and I spent a long time choosing these images that are edgy and galactic. Some people relate to these images as raw and others as inspiring. However they speak to you, they will cut through the mind and allow you to communicate with your creative voice. I've also found them healing. They speak to me as the desert speaks to me: raw, intense, open, direct and forceful. The desert energy always forces me to show up exactly as I am. It brings me to a place of mindfulness and is a perfect place for healing as it strips away any illusions I may have. These images represent that same energy and have helped me tap into the telepathic and intuitive parts inside of myself; into the part of me that is both a tiny speck in the cosmos and the largest molecule of all there is. I hope that this creative process also bring you whatever inner shift you most desire.

This coloring your book can be used a stand-alone or as an adjunct to the SPARK series of books. Find out more at TheSpark.love

With Love,
Michelle
Author and Creator of SPARK:
The Radically Authentic Life Series

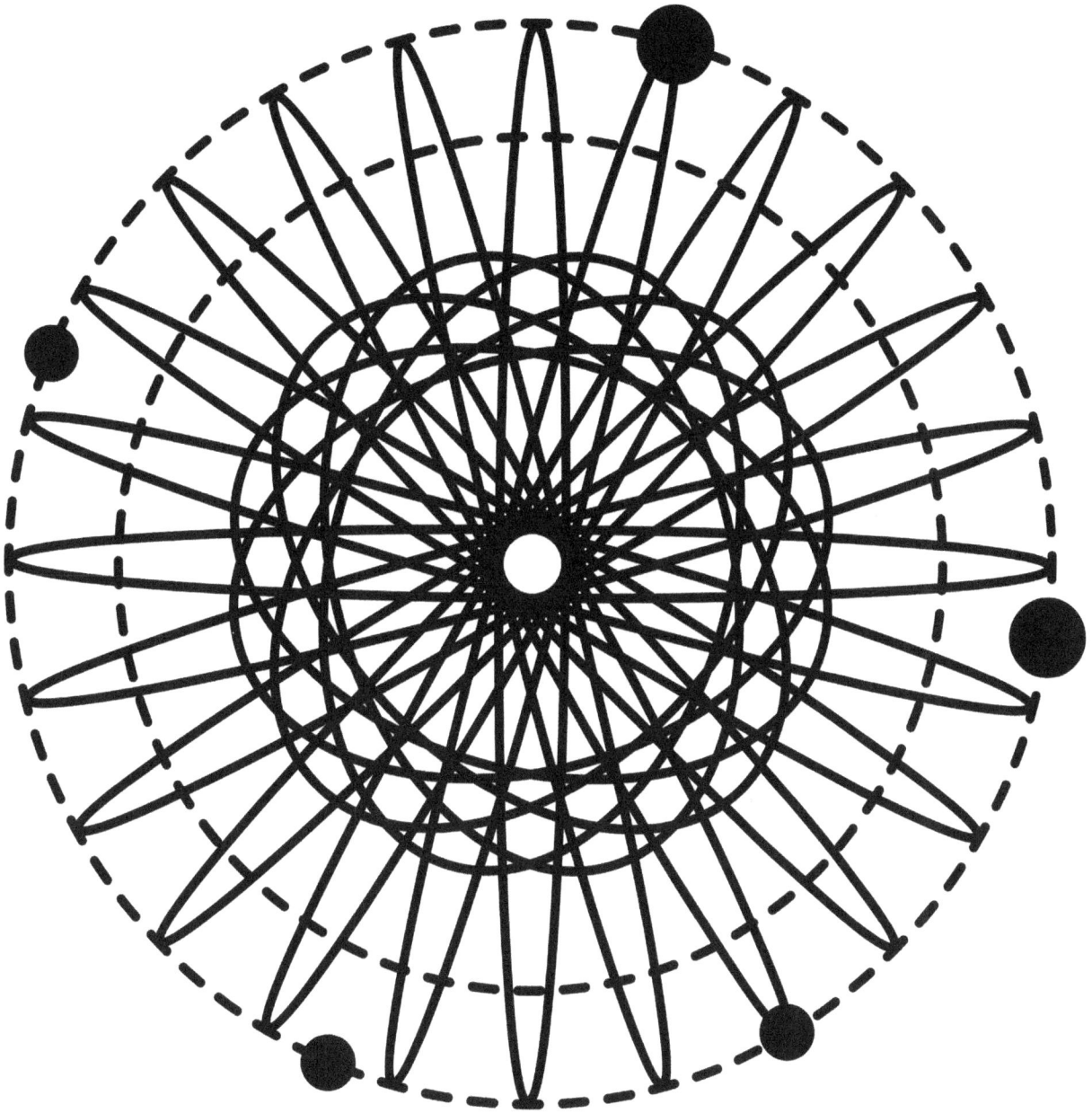

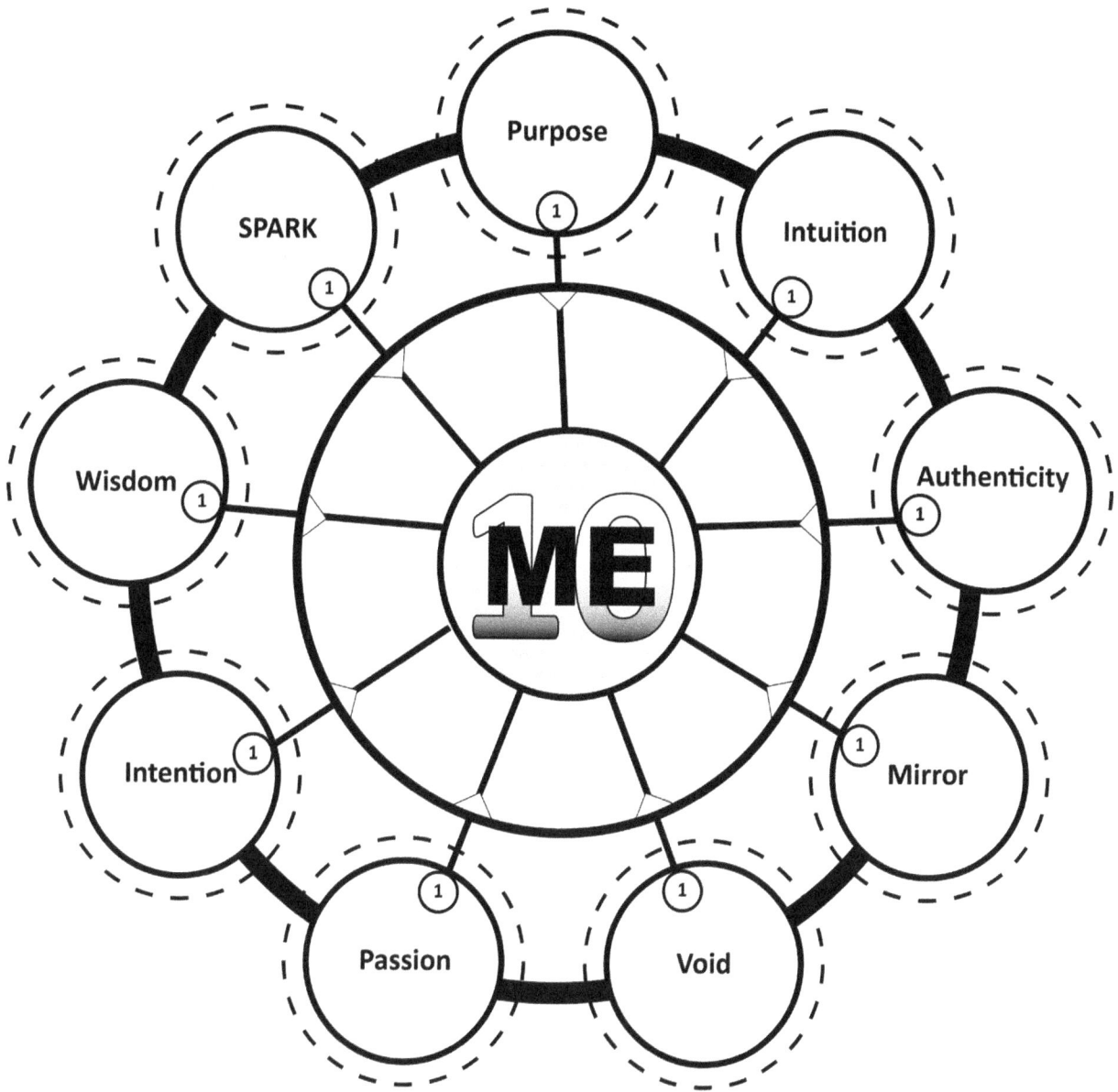

EARTH

WATER

ME

AIR

FIRE

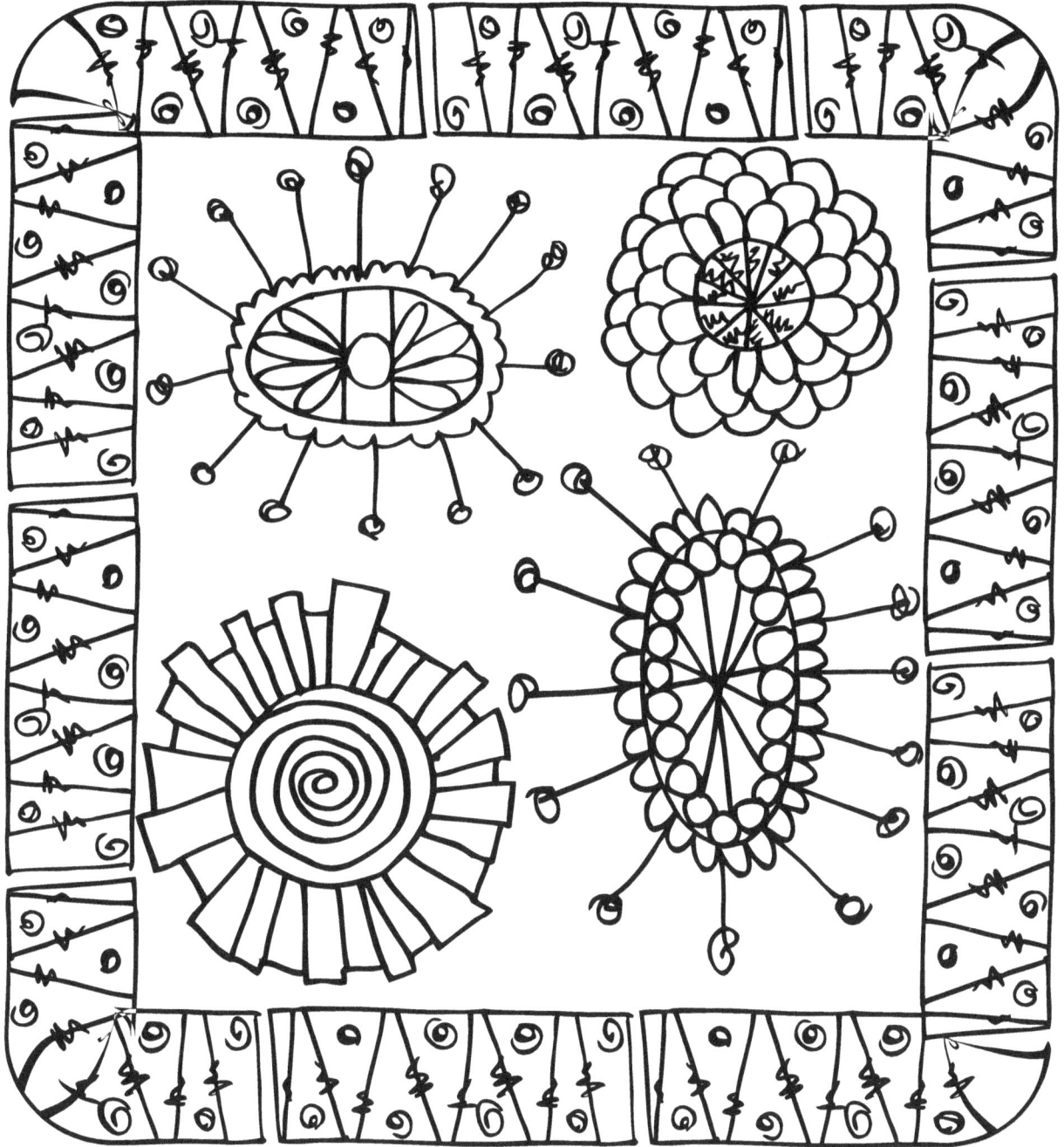

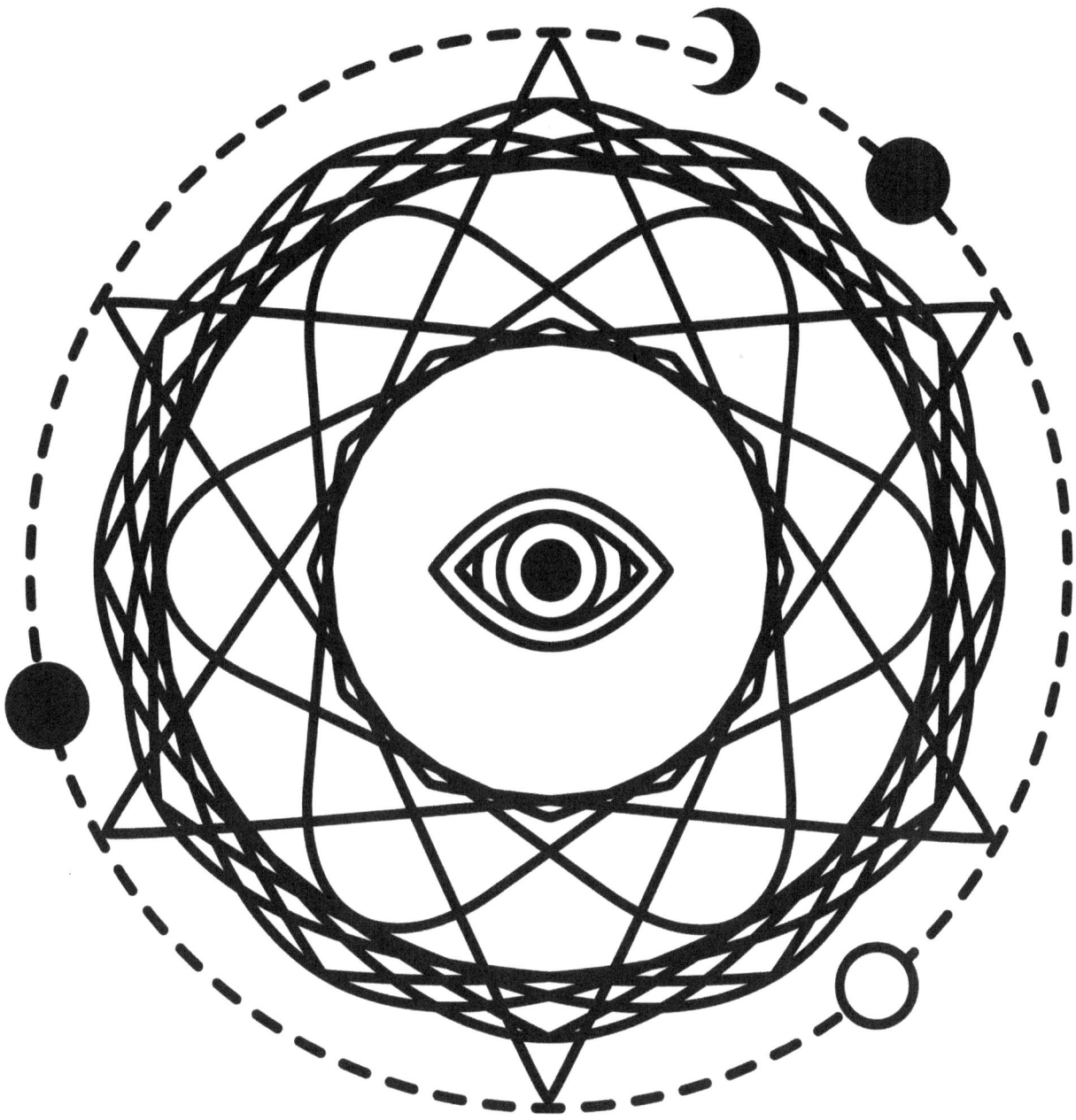

SPARK